Securing a Level 4 Mathematics

Hilary Koll and Steve Mills

Contents

RISING STARS

Rising Stars UK Ltd.
7 Hatchers Mews, Bermondsey Street, London SE1 3GS
www.risingstars-uk.com

Published 2010
Reprinted 2011, 2012, 2013

Authors: Hilary Koll and Steve Mills
Consultant Maths Publisher: Jean Carnall
Text design: Laura de Grasse
Typesetting: Ray Rich
Artwork: David Woodroffe
Cover Design: Burville-Riley Partnership

British Library Cataloguing in Publication Data.
A CIP record for this book is available from the British Library.

ISBN: 978-1-84680-718-3

Printed by Craft Print International Limited, Singapore.

Using  Shine!

This book will help you secure a level 4 in maths and focuses on key areas that pupils working at level 3 and level 4 often find difficult. Getting to grips with these areas will help you to move up a level.

1. Take a **System scan** to check out areas you need to work on.

2. **Go to page** … **Go to page** to find questions, games and activities to help.

3. **Plug in** to the topic with a quick warm up.

4. Use the **Chat room** to discuss mathematics with a partner.

5. **Power up** and work on the trickier parts of the topic.

6. Try a game in **Game play** for more practice.

7. Use the **Explore** activity to apply your knowledge.

Look at out for the photocopy masters for extra help, or for a larger version of a game.

1 Answer these questions.

a What is the **difference** between 70 and 22?

b What is the **sum** of 15, 35 and 29?

c Find the **product** of 3 and 22.

d **Share** 35 equally between 7.

e What is the **remainder** when 37 is divided by 5?

f What is the **total** of 9, 35 and 49?

g What number under 20 is a **multiple** of 3 and 4?

h What is the **total** of 0.2, 0.4 and 0.6?

i What is the **difference** between 10 and 3.8?

j Write all the **factors** of 8.

k What is 1.8 **doubled**?

l What is **half** of 3.4?

m What is 2.8 **divided by** 4?

Go to pages 22, 44, 60

---

2 Use the fact in the box to help you answer these questions.

$$5 \times 7 = 35$$

a $5 \times 70 =$

b $500 \times 7 =$

c $0.5 \times 7 =$

d $5 \times 0.07 =$

e $0.05 \times 7 =$

f $5000 \times 7 =$

g $350 \div 7 =$

h $3.5 \div 5 =$

Go to pages 18, 22, 30, 40, 58

3 Answer these questions.

a $360° \div 2$

b $90° \times 4$

c $360° - 150°$

d $360° \div 4$

e $90° \times 3$

f $360° - 90°$

g $45° \times 2$

h $30° \times 3$

---

4 Find the prices of the items in the basket, using rounding to help you.

Shopping Basket – To Buy		Price	Quantity	Total price
a	pack of batteries	£5.99	4	£ _____
b	flashcard	£7.99	3	£ _____
c	ink cartridge	£8.98	5	£ _____

Go to pages 16, 30, 32

Unit 1 – System scan B

1 Which two numbers in the grid have:
   a a difference of 1.01?
   b a total of 1.12?
   c a sum of 5.2?
   d a difference of 1.39?

3.7	2.9	1.5
1.28	0.07	4.32
1.05	2.51	2.89

Go to pages 16, 18, 20, 22, 30, 38

2 Answer these questions.
   a What is 0.3 multiplied by 5?
   b How many lots of 0.7 are there in 2.8?
   c What is 2.4 divided by 4?
   d What is half of 0.3?
   e What is 5.4 divided by 9?
   f What is double 0.45?

3 Use the diagram to answer each question.

   a Find the difference between 48 and 92.

   48   88   92

   b Find the sum of 54 and 39.

                          +40

   54

   c Find the difference between the times 9:24 and 11:08.

   9:24   9:30   10:00   11:00   11:08

Go to pages 18, 22, 30, 58

4 Answer these questions.
   a 36 + 7   b 100 – 47   c 49 + 27   d 92 – 15
   e 54 + 37   f 34 + 68   g 76 + 25   h 87 – 19

ALL UNITS

5 A container holds exactly 1 litre.

How many millilitres is it holding when it is:
   a half full?   b a quarter full?
   c three-quarters full?   d one-tenth full?
   e one-fifth full?   f two-fifths full?
   g seven-tenths full?   h four-fifths full?

Go to pages 16, 18, 20, 22, 30, 38

Unit 2 – System scan

1 What is the value of the blue digit in each number?
    a 3837   **b** 36 261   **c** 408 747   **d** 7 884 236   **e** 9.24   **f** 3.05

2 Write these numbers in digits.
    a four thousand and eleven
    b twenty thousand and six
    c forty-three thousand and thirty
    d one million and one
    e five million, three hundred and six thousand and twenty-four

 Go to page 12

3 Round these numbers.
    a Round 7482 to the nearest 100.
    b Round 52 479 to the nearest 1000.
    c Round 48 924 to the nearest 100.
    d Round 48 937 to the nearest 1000.
    e Round 43 099 to the nearest 100.
    f Round 25 550 to the nearest 1000.

 Go to page 14

4 Round these decimals to the nearest whole number.
    a 3.53   **b** 0.93   **c** 47.48   **d** 12.71   **e** 34.52

 Go to page 16

5 Which of these questions have the answer 42?
    a 4.2 × 10   **b** 420 ÷ 100   **c** 42 000 ÷ 1000
    d 0.42 × 100   **e** 4200 ÷ 10

 Go to page 18

6 Write the missing numbers on these number lines.

a
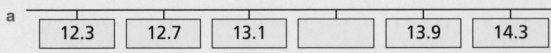

| 12.3 | 12.7 | 13.1 | | 13.9 | 14.3 |

b
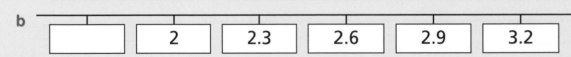

| | 2 | 2.3 | 2.6 | 2.9 | 3.2 |

Go to page 20

7 Answer these questions.
    a 4.7 + 3.3   **b** 6.7 − 2.9   **c** 2.14 + 3.65
    d 5.98 − 3.21   **e** 8.21 − 1.34   **f** 7.03 − 5.85

 Go to page 22

Unit 3 – System scan

1 Which pairs show the same time?

`16:20`

Twenty-five to four in the afternoon

`17:10`

Five to ten in the morning

`09:55`

Three thirty-five pm

Ten past five pm

Twenty past four in the afternoon

Go to page 24

2 Joe's sister was born on September 7th 1998.

On which day of the week was she born?

August 1998

Sun	Mon	Tues	Wed	Thu	Fri	Sat
						1
2	3	4	5	6	7	8
9	10	11	12	13	14	15
16	17	18	19	20	21	22
23	24	25	26	27	28	29
30	31					

3 Which numbers are missing?

  a 140 secs = 2 mins and ☐ secs **b** 3 weeks = ☐ days

  c 250 mins = ☐ hours and ☐ mins **d** 4 years = ☐ months

  e $1\frac{1}{2}$ days = ☐ hours **f** 2 hours and 25 mins = ☐ mins

Go to page 26

4 A DVD recorder is set to record 4 programmes with these start and end times. How long is each programme?

START	END	START	END
`2:45 PM`	`3:17 PM`	`1:36 PM`	`4:05 PM`
`7:19 AM`	`9:04 AM`	`9:48 PM`	`0:29 AM`

Go to page 28

5 Marco buys a book and a sunhat for £5.17.

  a What is the cost of the book?
  b How much change does he get from £20?

£3.29

Go to page 30

6 Safia buys 5 bananas, 1 melon and 3 pineapples.

Use a calculator to find the total cost.

36p each

£2.17 each

£1.99 each

Go to page 32

Unit 4 – System scan

1 What number is each arrow pointing to?

a   b   c   d

300   400   500

e   f   g   h

100   200

Go to page 34

or any other page in Unit 4 or Unit 5C

2 Estimate the length of each creature in millimetres.

a

b

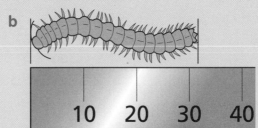

10   20   30

10   20   30   40

3 Estimate the mass shown on each scale.

a
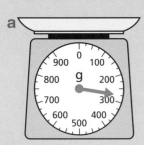

b
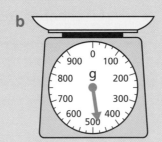

c
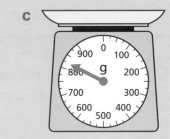

Go to page 36

or any other page in Unit 4

4 The scale shows how much an apple weighs

Approximately how many apples will you get in a 1 kg bag?

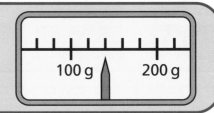

100 g   200 g

Go to page 38

or any other page in Unit 4

5 Write the measurements on the scales **in grams**.

a

b
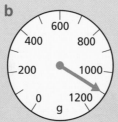

c

Go to page 40

or any other page in Unit 4

6 Write the measurements on the scales above **in kilograms**.

8

1 a Match each graph or chart with its name.

 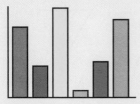  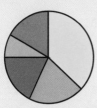

pie chart   pictogram   bar chart   line graph

Go to page 42

b What features are missing from each graph?

2 This graph shows the water level in a bath between 7pm and 8pm

Height of water in a bath

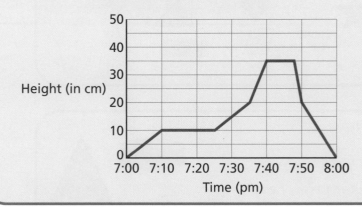

a What was the height of the water at 7:30?

b At approximately what times was the water level 25 cm?

c What might have happened at 7:10?

Go to page 44

Go to page 46

3 This pie chart shows the favourite colour chosen by 12 children.

How many children chose:
a green?   b blue?   c purple?

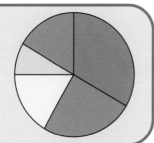

Go to page 48

4 This table shows the favourite TV programme of some children.

	Cartoons	Drama/stories	Educational	Quiz shows
Year 4	22	25	6	9
Year 5	16	14	19	16
Year 6	6	40	22	7

Go to page 50

a How many children chose cartoons altogether?
b How many children from Year 6 took part in the survey?

Unit 6 – System scan A

1 Look at these 2-D shapes.

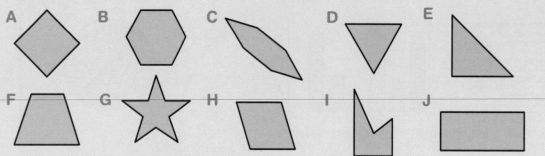

For each shape, write the number of:

a sides   b right angles   c lines of symmetry.

Go to page 52

2 Which of these shapes has been put in the wrong place?

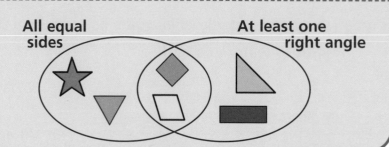

3 Answer these questions.

a What shapes are the faces of a cube?

b How many faces does a triangular prism have?

c How many vertices does a square-based pyramid have?

d How many vertices does a cuboid have?

e What is special about the edges of a cube?

f How many edges does a cylinder have?

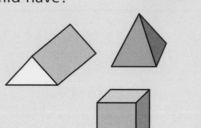

Go to page 54

4 Decide whether these statements are **true** or **false**.

a BG is parallel to AF.

b CD is perpendicular to DH.

c AE is parallel to DH.

d EC is perpendicular to CI.

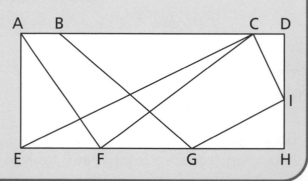

Go to page 56

Unit 6 – System scan B

1 Sam has started drawing a triangle with sides that are 6 cm and an angle that is 60°. Use a protractor and ruler to see if he is doing this correctly.

    a What has he done wrong?

    b Draw the triangle correctly on plain paper.

Go to page 58

2 Which of these shapes does not fold to make a cube?

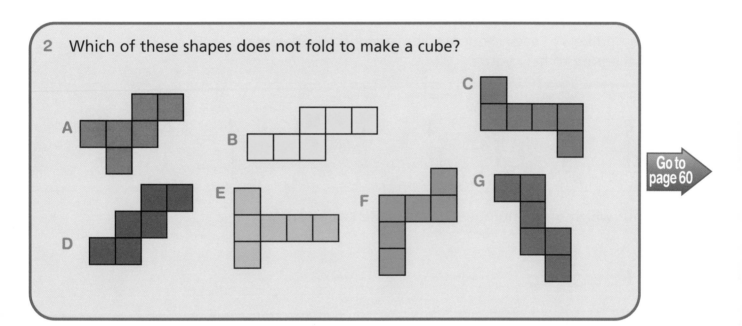

Go to page 60

3 Shape **A** has been changed in three ways.

- It has been reflected in the dotted line to make shape **B**.
- It has been rotated anticlockwise through 90° about one of its vertices to make shape **C**.
- It has been translated 4 squares to the left and 1 square up to make shape **D**.

What colours are shape **B**, shape **C** and shape **D**?

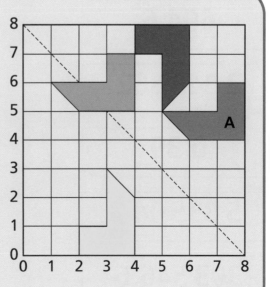

Go to page 62

Knowing the value of digits

Plug in

Write the next four numbers in each sequence.

a	1	10	100	1000	—	—	—	—
b	3000	300	30	3	—	—	—	—
c	0.07	0.7	7	70	—	—	—	—
d	0.002	0.02	0.2	2	—	—	—	—

Chat room

Read the numbers in each sequence above aloud to a partner.
Use this diagram to help you.

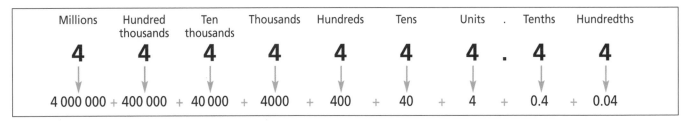

Millions	Hundred thousands	Ten thousands	Thousands	Hundreds	Tens	Units	.	Tenths	Hundredths
4	4	4	4	4	4	4	.	4	4
↓	↓	↓	↓	↓	↓	↓		↓	↓
4 000 000 +	400 000 +	40 000 +	4000 +	400 +	40 +	4 +		0.4 +	0.04

Talk about which of the numbers below is the largest.

Power up

1   Write the value of the red digit in each number.

a   604.6

b   5874.06

c   2 048 862

d   22 959.75

e   0.39

f   472 958.45

g   5 835 047

h   24 986.3

i   303 546.6

j   211 801.81

2 Work with a partner. You will need the cards from PCM 1. Choose several numbers on the grid below. For each number, find a card that contains a digit with that value.

20 000	3 000 000	8000	4 000 000	50
2 000 000	300 000	8	400	2000
40 000	8 000 000	70	10 000	600 000
500 000	7000	50 000	500	1
20	30 000	9 000 000	200 000	80 000
6000	90 000	100 000	7 000 000	50 000

3 Pick sets of four cards. Write down each set of numbers in order, starting with the smallest.

Game play
2 players

You will need: cards from PCM 1.

● Play a game of 'Snap'.
● Say 'Snap' when the two cards turned over have digits with the same value, e.g. 2583 and 16 784 both have the same tens digit, which has a value of 80.

Explore

Suggest two different numbers that lie between:

a   25 000 and 30 000
b   400 000 and 410 000
c   900 000 and 1 000 000
d   35 000 and 36 000
e   4 and 5
f   3.4 and 3.5

Rounding and using number lines

 Plug in

Round each number to the nearest 10.
Remember: your answer will be a multiple of 10.

a 48	b 92	c 35	d 128	e 482	f 708
g 135	h 658	i 205	j 9429	k 4806	l 3855

Chat room

These number lines show multiples of 100. With a partner, work out where the red numbers should go.

17   534   293   4483   4732   4049   17 432   17 599   17 951

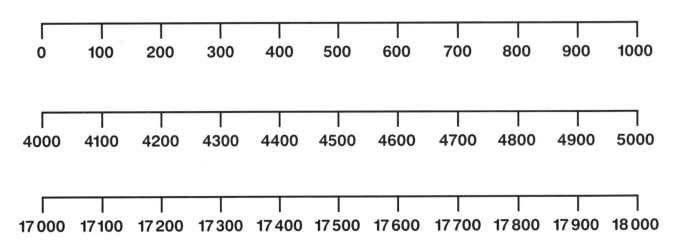

Talk about how to round each number to the nearest 100. How can the number lines help?

 Power up

1   Round each number to the nearest **100**. Remember: your answer will always be a multiple of 100.

a 3517	b 2948	c 7325	d 4688	e 3796
f 7033	g 38 250	h 48 629	i 39 910	j 32 078

2   Which digit in each number helps you decide which multiple of 100 to round to?

3 Round each number to the nearest **1000**. Remember: your answer will always be a multiple of 1000.

| a | 8517 | b | 3948 | c | 27 325 | d | 34 688 | e | 33 796 |
| f | 73 033 | g | 38 550 | h | 48 629 | i | 30 910 | j | 36 099 |

4 Which digit in each number helps you decide which multiple of 1000 to round to?

Game play
2 players

- Take turns to choose a calculation from the grid below.
- Both players estimate the answer by rounding the numbers. You have 20 seconds to do this.
- Use a calculator to work out the answer. The player whose estimate is closest to the answer wins a point.
- The winner is the first player to reach 6 points.

27 × 31	326 + 217	34 × 19	9637 – 393
364 ÷ 7	584 × 2	27 × 31	5746 ÷ 2
957 + 265	1113 – 491	198 ÷ 6	357 × 2
38 × 51	234 ÷ 6	828 + 176	5482 ÷ 2
54 × 29	648 + 159	65 × 13	695 – 178
388 ÷ 7	685 × 2	3562 + 378	2476 ÷ 2
897 + 382	5411 – 644	306 ÷ 9	613 × 2
57 × 98	207 ÷ 3	474 + 957	4856 ÷ 2

Explore

Match the price of each gadget with a description.

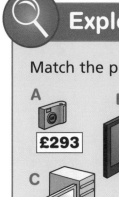

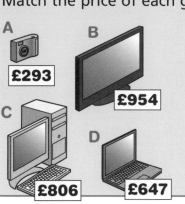

A £293

B £954

C £806

D £647

1 If you bought two of them you'd need just over £1600.

2 Four of them would cost less than £1200.

3 Two of them would cost about £1300.

4 You would get about £50 change from one thousand pounds.

Rounding decimals and calculating mentally

Plug in

Write a decimal number for each arrow.

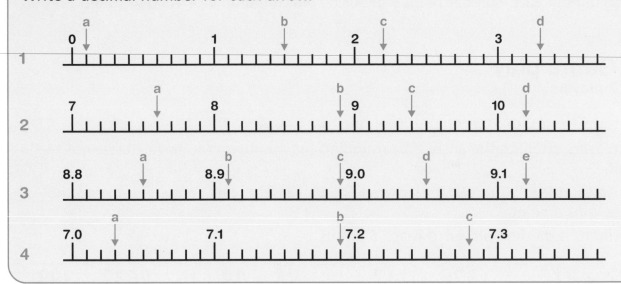

Power up (1)

Round these decimals to the nearest **whole number**.
Remember: your answer will always be a whole number.

| a | 5.1 | b | 4.8 | c | 7.3 | d | 15.7 | e | 22.3 | f | 7.11 | g | 6.95 |
| h | 12.39 | i | 8.61 | j | 125.7 | k | 43.52 | l | 34.50 | m | 375.32 | n | 49.71 |

Game play
2 players

- Both players write these numbers on a piece of paper:

  £7 £8 £9 £10 £11 £12 £13 £14

- Take turns to choose any two amounts from the grid.

- Round them to the nearest pound and estimate the sum of the two amounts. If you can, cross off the estimated result in your list.

- The winner is the first player to cross off all the estimates on their list.

£3.76	£4.25	£5.50
£8.12	£6.49	£2.40
£7.24	£6.81	£5.72
£3.35	£4.57	£6.50
£3.29	£2.77	£7.41
£1.87	£2.79	£4.26
£5.45	£7.50	£1.50
£3.58	£4.21	£3.53
£5.60	£5.36	£6.07
£6.10	£7.29	£5.35

Power up (2)

Look at these calculations with a friend. Work together to round each decimal and work out an approximate answer for each question.

a 53 × 8.8 =   b 6.4 + 5.7 =   c 64 ÷ 2.9 =

d 8.8 − 2.9 =   e 7.1 × 2.9 =   f 5.3 × 4.7 =

g 1.64 + 8.52 + 7.39 =   h 1.96 × 6.18 =   i 9.73 ÷ 1.96 =

Now use a calculator to answer the questions and see how close your estimates were.

 Chat room

With a partner, make up three more questions using the numbers on the cubes below. Work out an approximate answer for each. Give your questions to the rest of the group and talk about how to find the approximate answers.

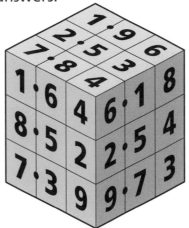

 Explore

Find the prices of the items in the basket, using rounding to help you.

Shopping Basket – To Buy		Price for 1:	Quantity:	Total price:
1	pack of batteries	£6.99	4	£ _____
2	flashcard	£8.99	3	£ _____
3	ink cartridge	£9.98	6	£ _____
4	USB drive	£7.97	3	£ _____

Multiplying and dividing by 10, 100 and 1000

Plug in

Answer these questions as quickly as you can.

a 4 × 10   b 6 × 10   c 0 × 10   d 3 × 10   e 10 × 10   f 9 × 10   g 2 × 10

Chat room (1)

Talk to a partner about which contestant you think is giving the correct answer.
Explain how you know.

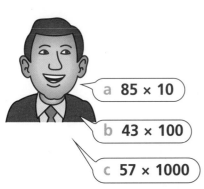
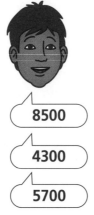

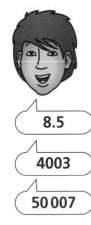

a 85 × 10   8500   850   8.5

b 43 × 100   4300   43 000   4003

c 57 × 1000   5700   57 000   50 007

Can you explain what happens to the digits of a number when you
multiply by 10, 100 or 1000?

Millions	Hundred thousands	Ten thousands	Thousands	Hundreds	Tens	Units	•	Tenths	Hundredths
							•		

Power up (1)

Answer these questions.

a   98 × 10   b   56 × 100   c   12 × 1000

d   143 × 10   e   209 × 100   f   71 × 1000

g   0.5 × 10   h   0.9 × 100   i   0.8 × 1000

Game play
2 players

- Play the game on PCM 2 with a partner. You will need to cut out the cards.

Chat room (2)

Talk to a partner about which contestant you think is giving the correct answer to each question. Explain how you know.

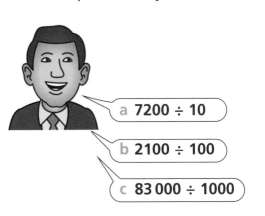 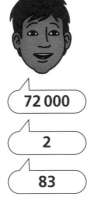 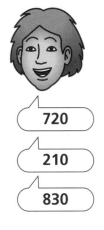 

a 7200 ÷ 10	72 000	720	72
b 2100 ÷ 100	2	210	21
c 83 000 ÷ 1000	83	830	8.3

Can you explain what happens to the digits of a number when you divide by 10, 100 or 1000?

 ## Power up (2)

Answer these questions.

a 980 ÷ 10

b 5600 ÷ 100

c 12 000 ÷ 1000

d 1400 ÷ 10

e 2000 ÷ 100

f 70 000 ÷ 1000

g 21 ÷ 10

h 8 ÷ 100

i 3500 ÷ 1000

j 0.1 ÷ 10

k 64 ÷ 100

l 750 ÷ 1000

Explore

Use the fact in the green box to help you answer these questions.

$$6 \times 7 = 42$$

a $6 \times 70 =$

b $600 \times 7 =$

c $0.6 \times 7 =$

d $6 \times 0.07 =$

e $0.06 \times 7 =$

f $6000 \times 7 =$

g $6 \times 700 =$

h $6 \times 0.7 =$

i $60 \times 70 =$

j $0.6 \times 70 =$

k $600 \times 0.07 =$

l $60 \times 0.07 =$

m $4.2 \div 7 =$

n $4.2 \div 0.6 =$

o $420 \div 7 =$

p $0.42 \div 6 =$

Understanding decimal sequences

 Plug in

Copy and complete these sequences.

1 Count on in tenths: 0.1 0.2 0.3 0.4 __ __ __ __ __ __ __ __ 1.3
2 Count on in tenths: 2.5 2.6 2.7 2.8 __ __ __ __ __ __ __ 3.7
3 Count on in hundredths: 3.75 3.76 3.77 3.78 __ __ __ __ __ __ __ __ 3.87
4 Count on in hundredths: 9.92 9.93 9.94 9.95 __ __ __ __ __ __ __ __ 10.04

 Chat room

Explain to a partner what you know about the numbers in each pair.

| 8 | 8.0 | | 101 | 101.0 | | 3.7 | 3.70 |

 Game play

Find the routes through the maze, counting on or back in equal-sized steps.

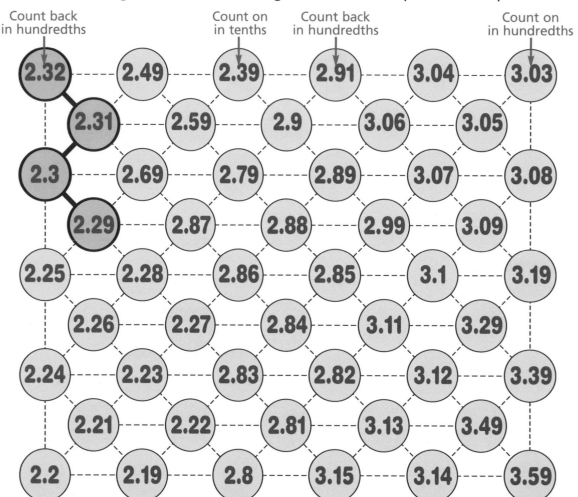

20

Power up

Work out the missing numbers.

a | 7.5 | 8 | 8.5 | 9 | 9.5 | ⬚

b | 0.8 | 1 | 1.2 | 1.4 | ⬚ | 1.8

c | 13.3 | 13.7 | 14.1 | ⬚ | 14.9 | 15.3

d | ⬚ | 10 | 10.3 | 10.6 | 10.9 | 11.2

e | 8.25 | 8.5 | 8.75 | ⬚ | 9.25 | 9.5

f | ⬚ | 6.05 | 6.1 | 6.15 | 6.2 | 6.25

 Explore

1 The measurements below are lengths of wood in Mr Brown's workshop. Help him sort them into the following groups.

● Less than 0.5m
● Between 0.5m and 1m
● Between 1m and 1.5m
● Between 1.5m and 2m
● Between 2m and 2.5m
● More than 2.5m

1.3 m	0.75 m	2.7 m	1.6 m	0.93 m	3.02 m
2.09 m	4.01 m	0.49 m	1.51 m	2.42 m	1.8 m
0.46 m	2.24 m	1.97 m	0.8 m	1.11 m	1.83 m
0.09 m	2.67 m	5.02 m	1.34 m	2.28 m	0.65 m
1.32 m	2.3 m	1.64 m	3.2 m	1.82 m	3 m

2 Now write the blue measurements in order of size, starting with the smallest.

Calculating with decimals

 Plug in

Answer these questions.

1 What is the **total** of 0.2, 0.4 and 0.6?   2 What is 2.6 **doubled**?

3 What is **half** of 3.2?   4 What is the **difference** between 10 and 2.8?

5 What is 0.3 **multiplied** by 4?   6 How many **lots of** 0.7 are there in 2.1?

7 What is 2.8 **divided** by 4?   8 What is **half** of 0.3?

 ## Chat room (1)

With a partner, choose two numbers from the grid.

- Find the **total** of the two numbers.
- Talk about how you can work out the answer.
- Do this five times. Do you use the same strategy each time?
- Did you make any notes?

3.7	2.9	1.5
1.28	0.07	4.32
1.05	2.51	2.89

 ## Game play
2 players

You will need: 2 counters, 2 coloured pencils and a dice.

- Play the game on PCM 3. Take turns to place two counters in different positions on the ring.
- Roll the dice and move one of the counters on. Find the total of the two numbers that the counters are on.
- If the total is in the grid at the bottom of the sheet, colour it in your colour.
- Keep rolling the dice, moving the counter of your choice each time.
- The winner is the first player to get 5 of their own colour in a line.

 ## Chat room (2)

With a partner, choose two numbers from the grid.
- Find the **difference** between the two numbers.
- Talk about how you can work out the answer.
- Do this five times. Do you use the same strategy each time?
- Did you make any notes?

5.68	4.07	8.52
3.7	2.9	4.5
6.05	2.51	2.89

Power up

Find difference between each pair of numbers.

a   4.7 and 9.3   b   2.89 and 1.54   c   6.7 and 5.99   d   6.17 and 4.35

e   7.2 and 1.15   f   6.43 and 2.3   g   8.65 and 1.5   h   4.29 and 2.9

i   8.01 and 3.99   j   3.5 and 1.72   k   8.08 and 5.76   l   7.03 and 5.85

Explain to a friend the different strategies you used for each calculation.

Explore

Here are the lengths of some pieces of furniture.

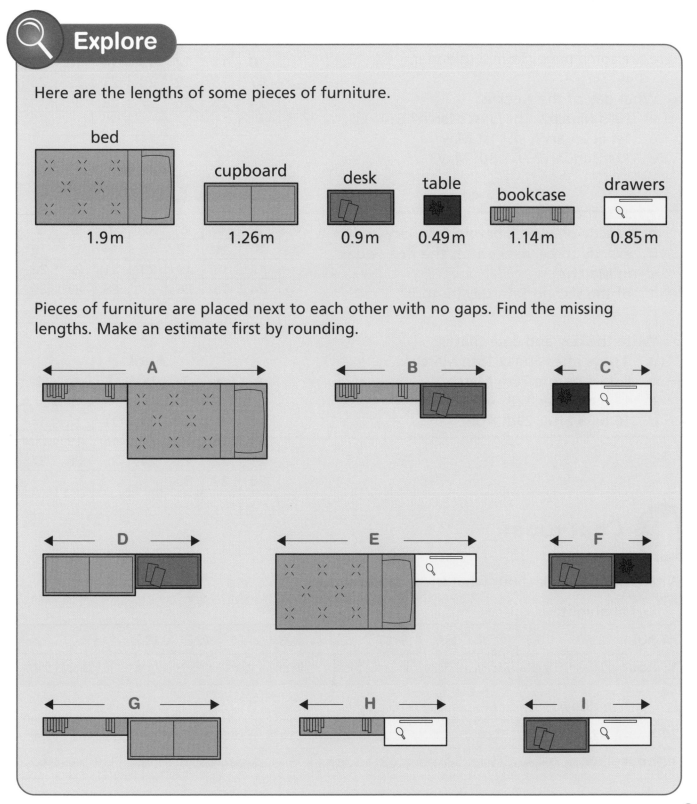

Pieces of furniture are placed next to each other with no gaps. Find the missing lengths. Make an estimate first by rounding.

Plug in

Use the loop cards on PCM 4 as a warm-up activity.

Power up

Here are some pages from a calendar.

1 What day of the week is:
  a 23rd March? b 31st March?
  c 1st February? d 1st May?
  e 31st January? f 8th May?

2 What is the date:
  a exactly one week before February 2nd?
  b exactly three weeks after the first Friday in March?
  c of the second Saturday in April?

3 Write the day and date that is:
  a 3 days after Friday 15th March.
  b 6 days before 26th March.
  c 11 days after 12th April.
  d 16 days after 29th April.

February

S	M	T	W	T	F	S
					1	2
3	4	5	6	7	8	9
10	11	12	13	14	15	16
17	18	19	20	21	22	23
24	25	26	27	28	29	

March

S	M	T	W	T	F	S
					1	2
3	4	5	6	7	8	9
10	11	12	13	14	15	16
17	18	19	20	21	22	23
24	25	26	27	28	29	30
31						

April

S	M	T	W	T	F	S
	1	2	3	4	5	6
7	8	9	10	11	12	13
14	15	16	17	18	19	20
21	22	23	24	25	26	27
28	29	30				

Chat room

With a partner, talk about what these tables show.

midnight

24-hour	00:00	01:00	02:00	03:00	04:00	05:00	06:00	07:00	08:00	09:00	10:00	11:00
12-hour	12:00am	1:00am	2:00am	3:00am	4:00am	5:00am	6:00am	7:00am	8:00am	9:00am	10:00am	11:00am

midday

24-hour	12:00	13:00	14:00	15:00	16:00	17:00	18:00	19:00	20:00	21:00	22:00	23:00
12-hour	12:00pm	1:00pm	2:00pm	3:00pm	4:00pm	5:00pm	6:00pm	7:00pm	8:00pm	9:00pm	10:00pm	11:00pm

▶ **Game play**

You will need: a counter.

- Place a counter on START.
- Find the matching time and move to it, placing a counter on the card you have just left.
- Repeat until all cards have a counter on them.
- Which is the final card that does not have a matching time?
- Write that time in 24-hour clock time.

START	**02:05**	**10:45**	**17:50**	**15:30**
Half past three in the afternoon	Quarter past 12 at lunchtime	Twenty past seven pm	Twenty past seven in the morning	Five minutes to nine pm
19:20	**01:13**	**20:55**	**23:45**	**03:30**
Three thirty a.m.	Five past two p.m.	Ten to six in the evening	Quarter to eleven in the morning	Twenty past six in the evening
07:20	**12:15**	**18:20**	**05:50**	**14:05**
Ten to six a.m.	Quarter to midnight	Thirteen minutes past one at night	Five past two am	Quarter to eleven in the evening

 🔍 **Explore**

Here is part of a bus timetable. Write four questions about it. Make sure you know the answers to your questions! Notice that 24-hour clock times are used.

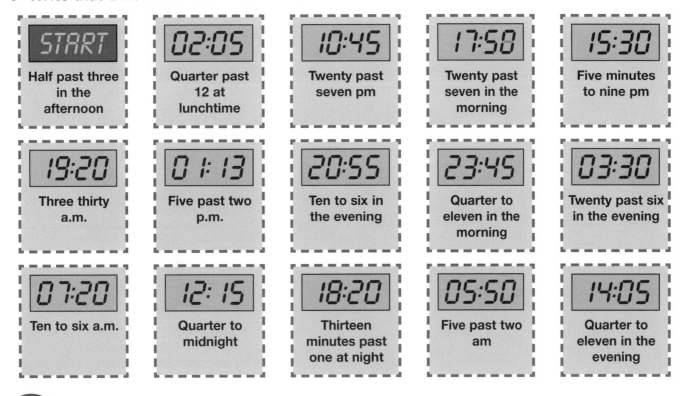

Kingston ● Long Finton ● Farmoor

Monday to Friday									
Kingston Townhead	1755	1810	1825	1855	1925	2025	2125	2225	2318
Abigail Street	|	|	|	|	|	|	|	|	|
Newford	1805	1818	1833	1903	1933	2033	2133	2233	2326
Stoke Cross	1812	1824	1839	1909	1939	2039	2139	2239	2332
Hurst Cross	1818	1830	1845	1915	1945	2045	2145	2245	2338
Long Finton Bus Station	1831	1838	1857	1923	1957	2057	2157	2257	2346
Borley Heath		1841		1907		2007	2107	2207	2307
Farmoor, Town Square		1849		1915		2015	2115	2215	2315

Your teacher will use the questions for a quiz.

Converting between units of time

 Plug in

1 Count on in 7s from 0 to 70.

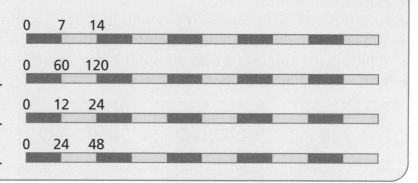

2 Count on in 60s from 0 to 600.

3 Count on in 12s from 0 to 120.

4 Count on in 24s from 0 to 240.

 Power up

This microwave has four buttons:

| +1 min | +1 sec |
| +10 mins | +10 secs |

Which buttons would you press to set the microwave for each of these times?

1	90 seconds	2	61 seconds
3	70 seconds	4	120 seconds
5	600 seconds	6	152 seconds
7	200 seconds	8	671 seconds

Try to use as few button presses as possible.

 Game play
2 players

You will need: the cards from the top of PCM 5.

- Play 'Snap' with a partner. Which microwave times are the same?
- Use the counting stick at the top of PCM 5 to help you.

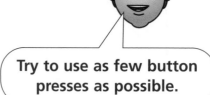

150 seconds
=
$2\frac{1}{2}$ minutes

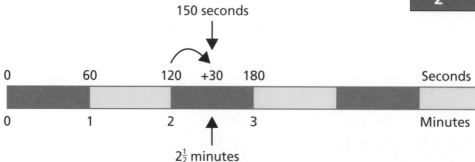

Chat room

Talk to a partner about these messages.

'Footie mad'

I read that Rooney has scored 10 goals in 470 minutes so far this season! Does anyone know many hours this is?

'Semour Flicks'

The latest Brad Pitt movie is 137 minutes long. His last one was 2 hours and 12 minutes. Which film is longer?

Mobile Mania

Contract deal – 800 minutes of free calls
Only £37 per month

'NZBaby'

I'm flying out to New Zealand on Monday. The flight is $27\frac{1}{2}$ hours long!!! The flight leaves at 7:15pm. What time will it be in the UK when I land?

Explore

Write down your date of birth.

Use a calendar to help you find your age in years, months and days.

Are you older or younger than these people?

1 I'm $10\frac{1}{2}$ years.

2 I'm 100 months.

3 I'm 600 weeks.

4 I'm 131 months

5 I'm 4000 days.

6 I'm 100 000 hours.

7 I'm 543 weeks.

8 I'm 3744 days.

9 I'm 6 million minutes.

10 I'm 10 years and 320 days.

11 I'm 127 months and 10 days.

Adding times and finding time differences

Plug in

Count on to continue these sequences.

a   3:32 3:37 3:42 __ __ __ __ __ __ 4:17

b   6:23 6:43 7:03 __ __ __ __ __ __ 9:23

c   12:10 12:25 12:40 __ __ __ __ __ 2:10

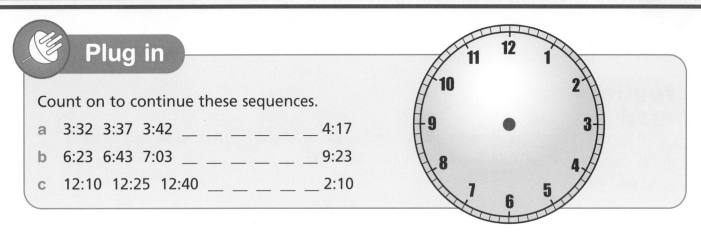

Chat room

Tell a partner how you could use these number lines to work out the difference between 9:23 and 11:13.

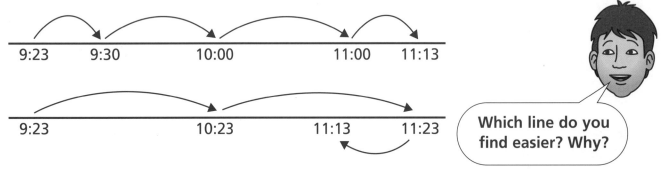

Which line do you find easier? Why?

Power up

This DVD recorder has been programmed to record five TV shows.

1   What is the length of each programme?

	Media	Ch.	Date	Start Time	End Time	Mode	Set-Top Channel
	Timer Record					0 min Free	
a	DVD	AV1	12/07 Sun	2:01 PM	2:31 PM	SP	OFF
b	DVD	AV1	12/07 Sun	2:15 AM	2:57 AM	SP	OFF
c	DVD	AV1	12/07 Sun	3:09 PM	5:40 PM	SP	OFF
d	DVD	AV1	12/07 Sun	6:10 AM	9:45 AM	SP	OFF
e	DVD	AV1	13/07 Mon	6:45 PM	7:25 PM	SP	OFF

⊙ OK   ⌘ Close

2   What is the total length of all the recorded programmes?

3 Some of these programmes are recorded on different days.
For how long is the recorder turned off between each recording?

Timer Record						0 min Free
Media	Ch.	Date	Start Time	End Time	Mode	Set-Top Channel
DVD	AV1	12/07 Sun	11:30 PM	11:59 PM	SP	OFF
DVD	AV1	13/07 Mon	4:00 AM	1:00 PM	SP	OFF
DVD	AV1	14/07 Tue	1:00 PM	3:30 PM	SP	OFF
DVD	AV1	15/07 Wed	9:00 AM	10:15 AM	SP	OFF
DVD	AV1	16/07 Thu	11:45 AM	12:00 AM	SP	OFF

⊙ OK   ☊ Close

Game play
2 players

You will need: the cards from the bottom of PCM 5.

- Set an analogue clock to 12:15.
- Player 1 picks a card and moves the clock time on that length of time.
- Player 2 tries to say the new time before the clock is set.
- Take turns. Always use the new time as your next start time.

Explore

These clocks show the times passengers arrive at an airport.
How long before each plane leaves?

a Flight B253a to Berlin Leaving at 13:35
☐ hours and ☐ minutes

b Flight B444a to Munich Leaving at 19:05
☐ hours and ☐ minutes

c Flight B945b to Nice Leaving at 02:20
☐ hours and ☐ minutes

d Flight B124b to Lisbon Leaving at 17:45
☐ hours and ☐ minutes

e Flight B111b to Malaga Leaving at 15:25
☐ hours and ☐ minutes

f Flight B754c to Athens Leaving at 23:50
☐ hours and ☐ minutes

Now write each length of time in just minutes.

Calculation and money problems

 Plug in

Answer these questions.

a £2.99 × 2	b £3.99 × 5	c £0.70 × 4	d £0.90 × 3
e £4.50 × 6	f £1.80 × 2	g £0.60 × 3	h £3.98 × 2
i £2.05 × 6	j £3.05 × 7	k £0.75 × 4	l £1.25 × 5

 Power up

Here are some greengrocer's prices.

Peaches 45p each	Brussels sprouts 50p for $\frac{1}{2}$ kg	Cherry tomatoes £1.25 per kg	Pineapples £1.20 each	Grapes £4.70 per kg	Potatoes £2.80 for a 5 kg bag	Cucumbers £0.80 each

Answer these questions, showing your working.

How much does it cost to buy:

a   2 peaches and a pineapple?

b $2\frac{1}{2}$ kg of Brussels sprouts?

c   2 kg of cherry tomatoes and a cucumber?

d $\frac{1}{2}$ kg grapes?

e   a 5 kg bag of potatoes and 4 peaches?

f   2 cucumbers and $\frac{1}{2}$ kg Brussels sprouts?

g   10 kg of potatoes?

h   5 peaches and 1 kg of cherry tomatoes?

 Chat room

Talk to a partner about how you could solve these problems.
Write number sentences to show what you would do.

Three nectarines cost 78p altogether. What is the cost of five nectarines?

Five oranges cost £1.20. How many oranges could I buy with 72p?

Four apples cost £1.80 altogether. What is the cost of three apples?

Game play
2 players

- Each player starts with £20.
- Take turns to choose items from the grid to buy.
- Work out how much to pay and subtract it from your amount.
- Cover the item with a counter to show it has been sold.
- The winner is the first player to run out of money!

12 stickers costing 30p per sticker	3 magazines costing £1.25 each	12 chocolate bars costing £1.80 for 6 bars	5 eye shadows costing 90p each
12 toy cars costing £2.50 for 4 cars	3 cans of cola costing 45p per can	2 kg of grapes costing £3.70 per kg	12 packets of crisps costing £1.50 for a pack of 4 packets
8 bananas costing 40p each	6 chocolate eggs costing 99p for 2 eggs	12 tomatoes costing 99p per pack of 6	7 pens costing 30p each
15 pencils costing 40p per pack of 3	8 tennis balls costing £1.99 for a pack of 4 balls	3 packets of sweets costing 75p per packet	2 footballs costing £1.95 each
7 erasers costing £0.40 each	3 CDs costing £1.55 each	4 rulers costing £1.25 each	8 frisbees costing £1.30 for a pack of 2 frisbees

Explore

Which person pays the least for each purchase and by how much?

a **8 litres of milk**

Theo buys 8 bottles at 55p per litre.
Li buys two 4-litre bottles at £1.95 per bottle.

b **12 bread rolls**

Theo buys 3 packs of 4 rolls at 89p per pack.
Li buys 4 packs of 3 rolls at 67p per pack.

c **24 bags of crisps**

Theo buys 3 packs of 8 bags at £1.65 per pack.
Li buys 2 packs of 12 bags at £2.99 per pack.

d **24 sausages**

Theo buys 4 packs of 6 at £1.05 per pack.
Li buys 3 packs of 8 at £1.45 per pack.

Using calculators for money problems

Plug in

Write the value of each red digit. For example: £4.49 _40p_

a £8.54　　　b £30.08　　c £22.78　　　　d £85.70　　　e £159.39

Power up

Here are the prices of some stamps.

	1st Class stamp – Letter	**41p**
	1st Class stamp – Large Letter	**66p**
	2nd Class stamp – Letter	**32p**
	2nd Class stamp – Large Letter	**51p**

1 Jess used a calculator to work out the price of five 1st Class Large Letter stamps. He keyed in 66 × 5 and the display showed 330. How much is this?

2 Raz used a calculator to work out the price of fifteen 2nd Class Letter stamps. He keyed in 15 × 0.32 and the display showed 4.8. How much is this?

3 Use a calculator to find out how much it costs to buy:

a 6 of these?

b 35 of these?

c 30 of these?

e 15 of these?

f 200 of these?

d 17 of these?

Chat room

Who is right and who is wrong?

1

A
A calculator shows the answer **4.2** to the question £1.40 × 3. This means 4 pounds and 2 pence.

B
No it doesn't! It means 4 pounds and 20 pence.

2

A
A calculator shows the answer **10.6666667** to the question £32 ÷ 3. This would be rounded to 10 pounds and 66 pence.

B
No it wouldn't. It would be rounded to 10 pounds and 67 pence!

Game play
2 players

You will need: a calculator and some counters.

- Each player copies this number line.

£6	£6.10	£6.20	£6.30	£6.40	£6.50	£6.60	£6.70	£6.80	£6.90	£7

- Take turns to pick a question from the grid below and do the calculation.
- Round the answer to the nearest 10p and cross this off your number line, if you can.
- Place a counter on the question in the grid to show it has been used.
- The winner is the player who has crossed off the most numbers on their number line.

£20.17 ÷ 3	£41 ÷ 6	£39.10 ÷ 6	£18.05 ÷ 3	£30.61 ÷ 5	£56.42 ÷ 9
£46 ÷ 7	£18.83 ÷ 3	£55 ÷ 9	£32.37 ÷ 5	£76.66 ÷ 11	£43.84 ÷ 7
£48.32 ÷ 8	£30.92 ÷ 5	£51.24 ÷ 8	£30.87 ÷ 5	£19.73 ÷ 3	£45.79 ÷ 7
£7 ÷ 3 × 3	£27.63 ÷ 4	£6 ÷ 7 × 7	£46.63 ÷ 7	£41.63 ÷ 6	£33.92 ÷ 5
£57.86 ÷ 9	£66.43 ÷ 11	£52.31 ÷ 8	£66.67 ÷ 11	£62.09 ÷ 9	£50.99 ÷ 8
£33.54 ÷ 5	£18.44 ÷ 3	£34.48 ÷ 5	£25.83 ÷ 4	£40.35 ÷ 6	£26.89 ÷ 4

Explore

Use a calculator to find the total of each set of prices and how much change you would get from £20.

a   65p, £2.65, £1.44, £3.89 and 27p

b , 99p, £8.54, £7.98, £1.06 and 50p

c   £3.70, £5.09, 73p, £2.94 and 9p

d   £3.93, £4.08, £3.66, 28p and 90p

Understanding scales and intervals

Plug in

1   Count on in steps of 10 from:

a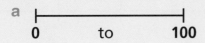
  0   to   100

b
  150   to   200

2   Count on in steps of 20 from:

a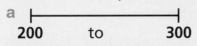
  200   to   300

b
  400   to   600

3   Count on in steps of 25 from:

a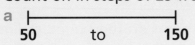
  50   to   150

b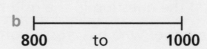
  800   to   1000

Chat room

Look at these rules for finding missing numbers on a scale.
Talk to a friend about them.
What number is missing from the box?

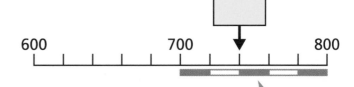

Step 1: Choose two adjacent given numbers and find the **difference** between them.	700 and 800 Difference is 800 − 700 = 100
Step 2: Count how many **intervals** (spaces) there are between these two numbers.	There are **5 intervals** (spaces) between 700 and 800.
Step 3: To find the size of each interval, divide the **difference** by the number of **intervals**.	100 ÷ 5 = 20
Step 4: Count up in steps of this size to check your working.	Each interval is worth 20, so count on in 20s from 700 to 800 to check.

Power up

Use the rules above to help you find the missing numbers.

1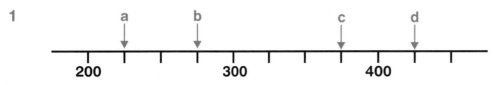

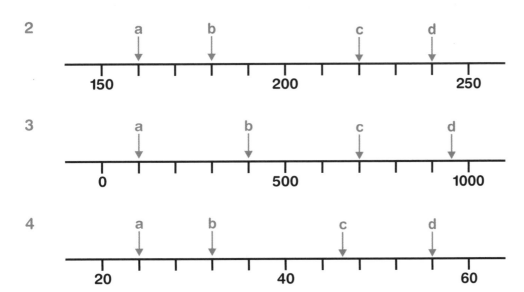

2

150   200   250

3

0   500   1000

4

20   40   60

▶ Game play

2 players: Blue and Red

- Each player finds the value of the arrowed marks in their colour, then works out the total of their readings.

- Which player has the highest total?

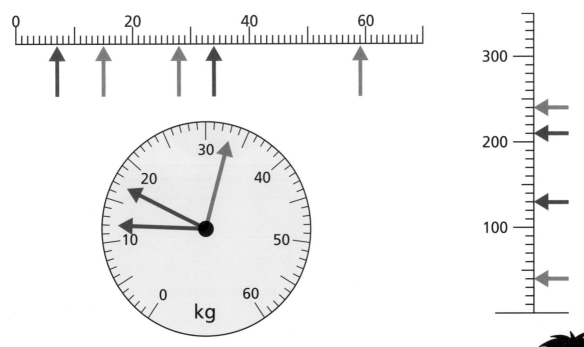

0   20   40   60

30
20   40
10   50
0   60
kg

300

200

100

 ## 🔍 Explore

Work with a partner. You will need measuring scales, tapes and containers. Measure the weights (masses), lengths and capacities of some classroom items.

Write each measurement including the unit. For example:
This mug has a capacity of 300 ml, a mass of 400 g and a height of 13 cm.

Reading scales and estimating

Plug in

1 What value lies exactly halfway between the numbers on each scale?

a
   0   20

b
  180   200

c
  1000   1500

d
  200   400

e
  50   150

f
  30   90

2 What value lies exactly a quarter of the way between the numbers on each scale?

Chat room

Talk to a partner about how you can estimate the diameter (the widest distance across) of these coins in millimetres.

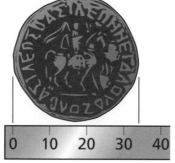

Power up

1 Estimate the lengths of these creepy crawlies in millimetres.

a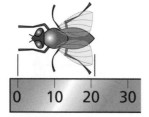

b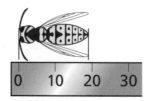

c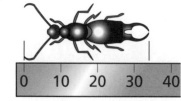

d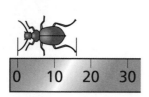

e

f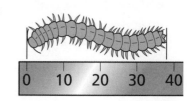

2   How heavy is each creature?

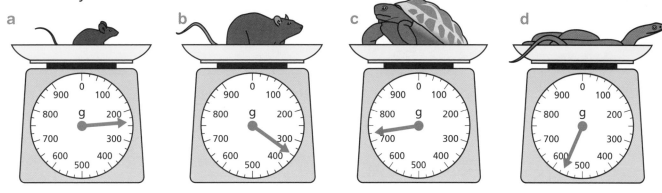

a   b   c   d

Game play
2 players

You will need: PCM 6, a dice and a blue coloured pencil each.

Explore

Record the readings on these scales. Remember to give the unit.

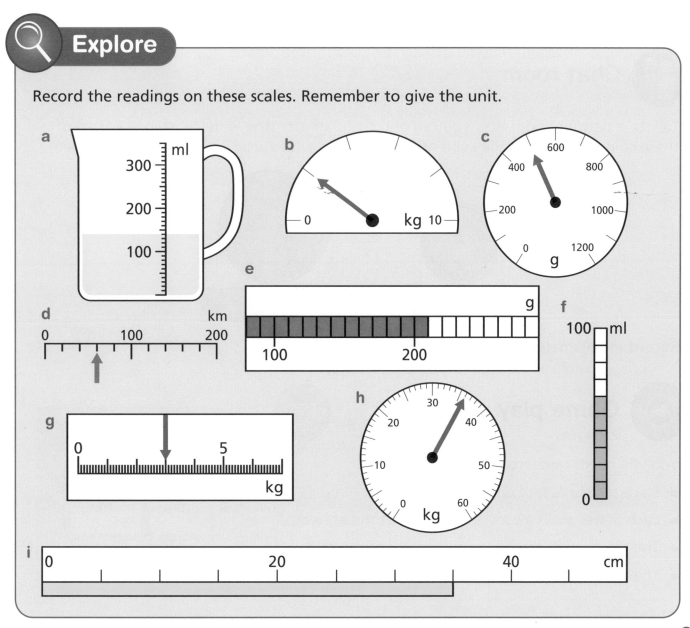

Solving measurement problems

Plug in

Find **one fifth** of these amounts.

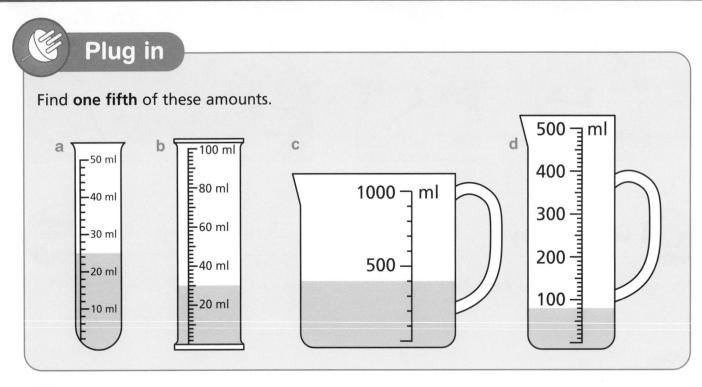

Chat room

Talk to a partner about how you can find the diameter (the widest distance across) of these coins. Notice that the coins are not lined up with zero.

Record the diameters in centimetres.

Game play
2 Players

You will need: cards from PCM 7.

- Place the cards face down on the table.
- Each player picks a card and works out the answer.
- The player with the larger answer keeps the card.
- The winner is the player with the most cards.

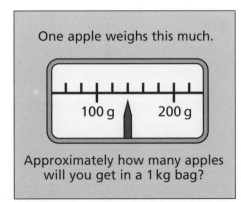

One apple weighs this much.

100 g   200 g

Approximately how many apples will you get in a 1 kg bag?

Power up

1 In each of these containers, some oil is floating on the top of some water. Work out how much oil is in each container.

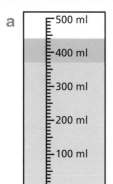 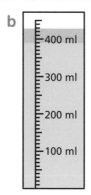 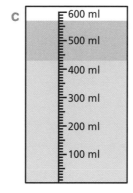

2 The liquid in the three test tubes is added to the measuring cylinders. What level will the liquid reach in each cylinder?

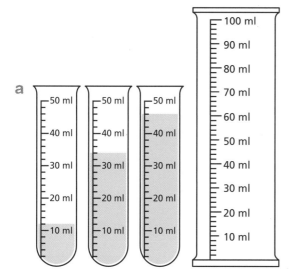 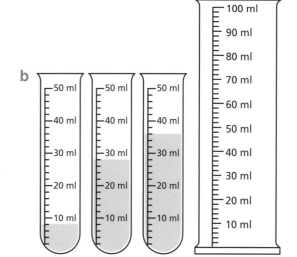

 Explore

Use the ruler to work out the diameter of each coin in centimetres.

Converting between units

Plug in

Answer these questions. Turn to page 18 if you need help.

a 4 × 1000	b 15 × 100	c 4000 ÷ 1000	d 19 × 1000
e 1.5 × 100	f 2500 ÷ 100	g 3500 ÷ 1000	h 1.8 × 1000
i 0.7 × 100	j 1750 ÷ 1000	k 50 ÷ 100	l 750 ÷ 1000

Chat room

Talk to a partner about the relationships between units of measurement and work out the missing numbers.

1 m = __ cm	1 kg = __ g	1 l = __ ml
1.5 m = __ cm	2.2 kg = __ g	1.75 l = __ ml
0.7 m = __ cm	0.95 kg = __ g	0.05 l = __ ml

Power up

1 Read these scales. Write the measurements in grams and then in kilograms.

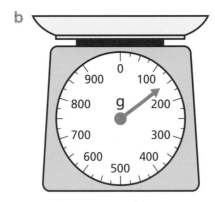

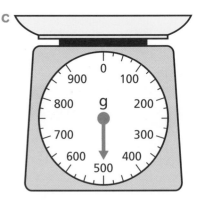

2 Write the value of each arrow in grams and then in kilograms.

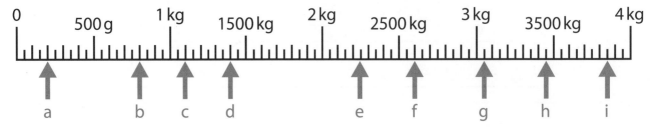

Game play

2 players

You will need: coloured cubes or counters.

- Choose a scale and then find the two matching readings.
- Place three counters or cubes in the same colour on them.
- How quickly can you cover all of them?

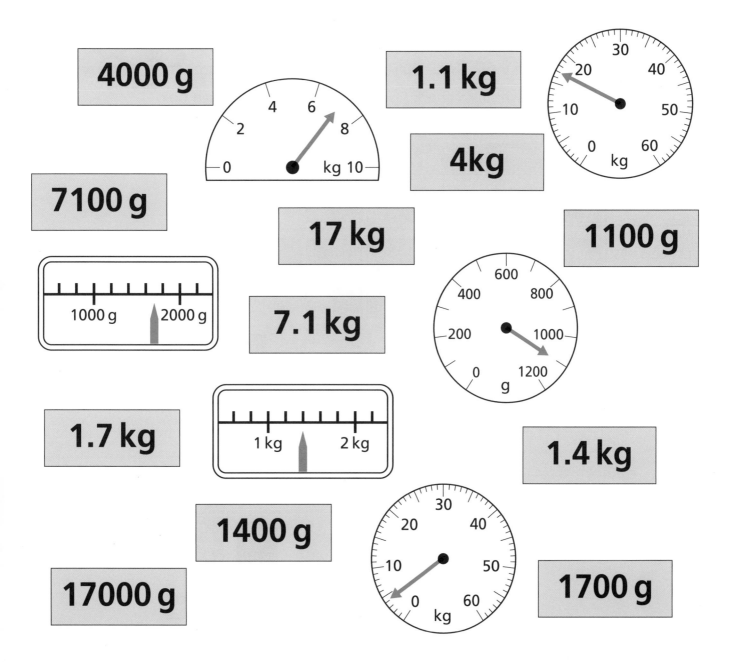

4000 g

1.1 kg

4 kg

7100 g

17 kg

1100 g

7.1 kg

1.7 kg

1.4 kg

1400 g

17000 g

1700 g

Explore

Measure the mass of some items in your classroom. Write each mass in grams and then in kilograms.

Recognising graphs and charts

 Plug in

Find the total of all the numbers: **a** from 1 to 10. **b** from 1 to 20.

 Chat room

Talk with a partner about what these charts and graphs are showing.

A sweet factory has a machine to check how many sweets are in each box.
This pictogram shows the number of sweets in each box.

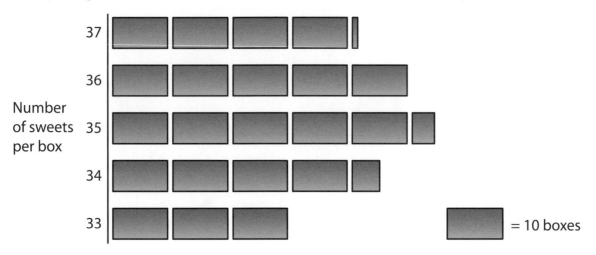

Number of sweets per box

$\square$ = 10 boxes

This bar chart shows the numbers of different-coloured sweets in one box.

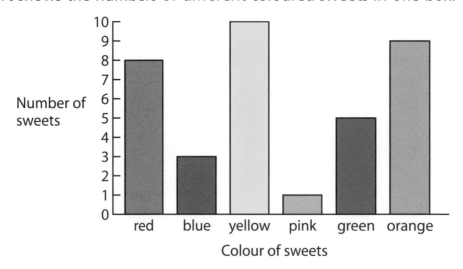

Number of sweets

Colour of sweets

This two-way table shows the approximate number of
boxes of sweets sold in England, Scotland and Wales in
a 3-month period.

	Jan	Feb	Mar
England	8000	9000	12000
Scotland	4000	6000	7000
Wales	4000	6000	9000

Power up

1 Work with a partner to write ten facts about the data on page 42.

2 Compare the bar chart on page 42 with the pie chart below. Do they show the same information? What is different about the way the information is shown in each chart?

3 Which of the two charts shows more clearly that:
   a the most common colour of sweets is yellow?
   b about a quarter of the sweets are orange?
   c there are about twice as many yellow sweets as green sweets?
   d almost half of the sweets are either red or orange?

4 Which of the charts on pages 42–43 has:
   a a scale?
   b a key?
   c cells?
   d sectors?

A pie chart to show the proportion of different-coloured sweets made in a factory

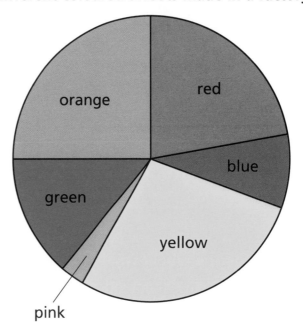

 Game play

Each pupil in a group writes 3 question cards about the information shown in the graphs for a class quiz. Make sure you write the correct answer too! Use questions starting with *Which was the most common … ? How many more … ? What fraction … ? How many altogether … ?*

 Explore

You could create your own survey about the colours of sweets in boxes, or your favourite colours of sweets and draw some charts or graphs to show the information. **Or** you could find out:

- how many pencils of each colour you have in the classroom.

- the number of cubes of different colours in a tray.

OR

- look at a website such as **www.smarties.co.uk** for data on the most popular sweet colour.

Interpreting graphs

 Plug in

Answer these questions.

1 What is the **difference** between 50 and 22?

2 What is the **sum** of 35, 35 and 29?

3 Find the **product** of 3 and 25.

4 **Share** 28 equally between 7.

5 What is the **remainder** when 24 is divided by 5?

6 What is the **total** of 9, 24 and 49?

7 Write all the **factors** of 6.

8 What number under 20 is a **multiple** of 3 and 5?

 Chat room

Talk to a partner about what the line graph shows. Can you work out what happened?

A private detective followed a suspect who was seen outside a police station at 8am in the morning and later went on to rob a bank. Use all the information given below to work out where the suspect went.

This line graph shows the distance of the suspect from the police station.

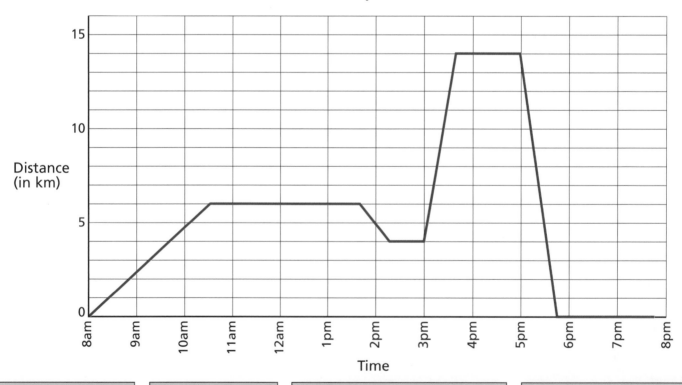

Distance from the police station

The train station is 4 km from the police station.

The bank is 14 km from the police station.

The police arrested the suspect at 5pm and drove him to the police station.

The suspect's mother's house is 6 km from the police station.

Power up

Answer these questions about the line graph on page 44.

1   At about what time did the suspect reach his mother's house?

2   About how long did he spend at his mother's house?

3   About how long did he wait at the station for a train?

4   Where was he at 12pm?

5   Where was he at 2pm?

6   Where was he at 4pm?

7   How far away from the train station is the bank?

8   How far did he travel in the police car?

Game play
2 players

You will need: cards from PCM 8.

● Work with a partner to answer the questions about this graph.

● This line graph shows a footballer's heart rate during an exercise session.

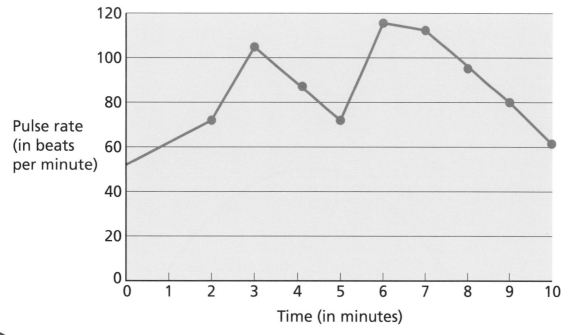

Heart rate during exercise

Explore

Look on the Internet or in newspapers or magazine for charts, tables and graphs.
Can you work out what each is showing?
Write some questions about the graphs and swap with a friend.

Plug in

1 Work out what number each red arrow is pointing to.

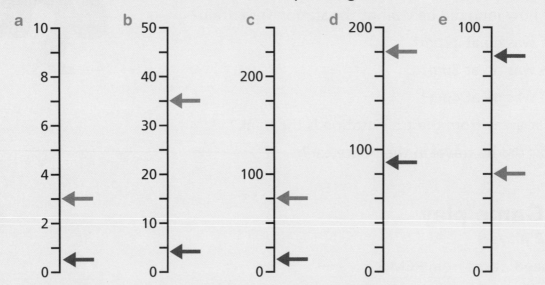

2 Now **estimate** the number each blue arrow is pointing to.

 ## Chat room

Two children are throwing stones into the sea. This line graph shows the height of the stones from the time they were thrown, to the time they landed in the water.

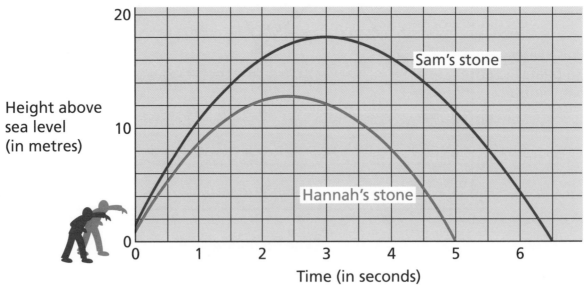

Talk to a friend about what this person is saying.

> **To find the height of a stone after 3 seconds, I draw a vertical line up from the 3 on the horizontal scale until I reach the curved line. I then draw a horizontal line from that point across to the other axis.**

Power up

1 From about what height was Hannah's stone at:
 a 4 seconds? **b** 3 seconds? **c** 5 seconds? **d** 1 second? **e** its highest point?

2 At about what height was Sam's stone at:
 a 1 second? **b** $1\frac{1}{2}$ seconds? **c** 5 seconds? **d** $5\frac{1}{2}$ seconds? **e** its highest point?

3 After about how many seconds was:
 a Sam's stone at its highest point? **b** Hannah's stone at its highest point?

4 After about how many seconds was Sam's stone at 10 metres above sea level?
 Give two answers to this question.

5 At what point was Sam's stone twice as high as Hannah's?

6 About how many seconds after Hannah's stone did Sam's fall into the water?

7 Rob says: **Both lines are wrong. They do not start at zero.** Do you think he is correct? Explain your answer to a partner.

 ## Game play
2 players

You will need: cards from PCM 9.

● Place the cards face down on the table.

● Each player picks a card and answers the question about the graph.

● The player with the larger answer wins both cards.

● The winner is the player with the most cards.

 ## Explore

Choose one of the cards from PCM 9 and tell a story about the way the bath was filled.

Think about:

● what time the bath began to be filled.

● whether the water went in slowly or quickly.

● how full the bath got.

● when the taps were turned off.

● whether any water was let out.

● what time the bath was emptied etc.

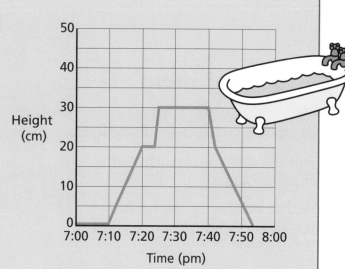

Plug in

What is:

1 one half of 24?   2 one quarter of 24?   3 one third of 24?
4 one twelfth of 24?   5 one sixth of 24?   6 one eighth of 24?

 Game play
2 players

You will need: a dice

- Before rolling, choose a colour from those in the circles below.
- Each roll the dice to find which circle you must each look at.
- Estimate what fraction of your circle is in your chosen colour and decide which player has the larger fraction. This player scores a point. If you both have the same amount, take another turn.
- Choose a new colour and roll again.
- The winner is the first player to reach 6 points.

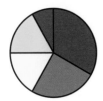  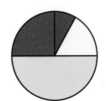   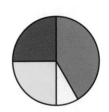

 Chat room

24 children have been on holiday.

This pie chart shows where the children stayed.

With a partner, make up four statements about this pie chart.

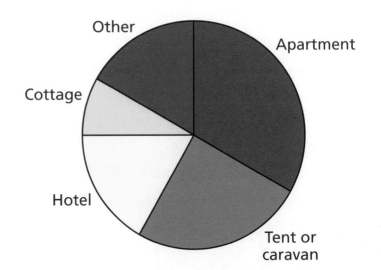

Power up

Look at the pie chart at the bottom of page 48.

1   Which was the most popular type of accommodation?

2   What fraction of the children stayed in:

   a   a tent or caravan?   b   a cottage or a hotel?   c   an apartment?

   d   a cottage?   e   a hotel?   f   another type of
                                                                         accommodation?

3   The pie chart shows information from 24 children.

   How many children stayed in:

   a   a tent or caravan?   b   a cottage or a hotel?   c   an apartment?

   d   a cottage?   e   a hotel?   f   another type of
                                                                         accommodation?

4   Explain to a partner how your answers would change if this chart showed information
    about the holidays of 48 children.

Explore

The bar chart shows which parts of the world a group of 110 children visited for
their holidays.

1   How many children spent
    their holiday in:

   a   Europe?

   b   Asia?

   c   Africa?

   d   North America?

2   How many more children
    went to:

   a   Europe than to
       Australasia?

   b   North America than
       to Africa?

   c   Europe than to Asia?

3   Write some of your own questions about the bar chart.

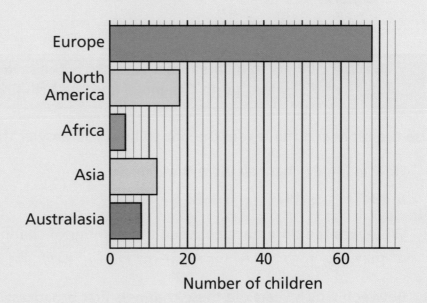

Solving data problems

Answer these questions. Draw number lines or make notes to help you.

a 26 + 7	b 37 − 19	c 39 + 7	d 49 + 8	e 92 − 15
f 54 + 17	g 34 + 38	h 94 − 29	i 73 + 18	j 85 − 28
k 17 + 45	l 94 − 39	m 76 − 17	n 66 + 25	o 97 − 19

 Power up

This table shows the number of TV channels broadcast in the UK for every 10 years between 1927 and 2007.

Year	1927	1937	1947	1957	1967	1977	1987	1997	2007
Number of channels	0	1	1	2	3	3	4	78	over 200

> **The first channel to be broadcast was BBC1. The second was ITV, the third BBC2, the fourth Channel 4 and the fifth Channel Five.**

Use the table and the text in the box to help you answer these questions.

1 How many TV channels were there in:

  a 1947?   b 1977?   c 1987?   d 1997?

2 What was the difference between the number of channels in:

  a 1947 and 1957?   b 1967 and 1977?   c 1977 and 1987?   d 1987 and 1997?

3 Between which years did these channels first broadcast?

  a BBC2   b ITV   c Channel 4   d BBC1   e Channel Five

4 What do you think happened between 1987 and 2007?

5 How many TV channels do you think there will be in 2017? Explain your thinking.

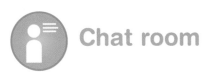 Chat room

Talk to a partner about what kind of chart or diagram you might draw to help you answer this question.

How many positive whole numbers less than 30 are multiples of 3 but are **not** multiples of 4?

Work together to find the answer.

 Game play
2 players

You will need: one copy of PCM 10 and paper, rulers and pencils.

● Follow the instructions and compare your diagrams for each round.

 Explore

Some children were asked to choose their favourite type of TV programme.

Here are the results of the survey.

	Cartoons	Drama/stories	Educational	Quiz shows
Year 4	27	32	6	15
Year 5	16	29	19	16
Year 6	6	40	22	12

Work out the answers to these questions using the data in the table.

1   How many children altogether chose:

   a cartoons?   b drama/stories?   c educational programmes?   d quiz shows?

2   How many children took part in the survey from:

   a Year 4?   b Year 5?   c Year 6?

3   How many children took part in the survey altogether?

Comparing and describing 2-D shapes

Plug in

There are 90 degrees in one quarter turn (a right angle). How many degrees in:

1 a half turn (2 right angles)?   2 a $\frac{3}{4}$ turn (3 right angles)?

3 a full turn (4 right angles)?   4 half a right angle?

5 one third of a right angle?   6 two thirds of a right angle?

Chat room

Talk to a partner about these shapes. Each pair has at least one thing in common. Think about names of shapes, numbers of sides, equal sides, angles, parallel lines, whether they are regular, lines of symmetry and so on.

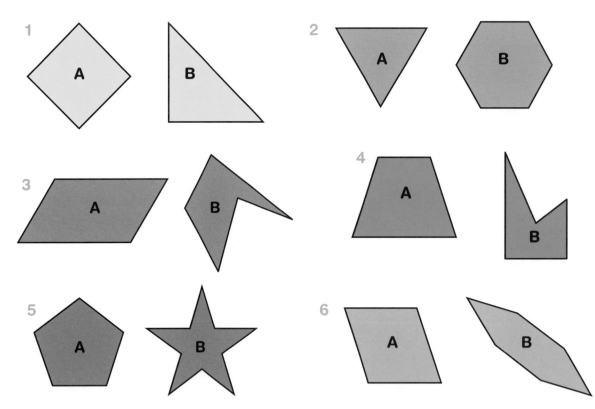

Power up

Choose three of the shapes above. Copy and complete this table.

Shape	Number of sides	Number of lines symmetry	Number of right angles

▶ Game play

2 players: blue and red

You will need: cards from PCM 11.

- Take turns to pick a card and decide where it would fit in each Venn diagram.
- Blue scores a point for each blue ring their shape fits into.
- Red scores a point for each red ring their shape fits into.
- You can score up to 4 points for each shape.
- The winner is the player with the highest score.

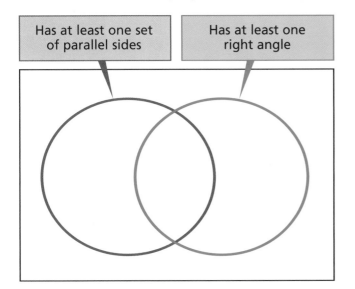

| Has at least one set of parallel sides | Has at least one right angle |

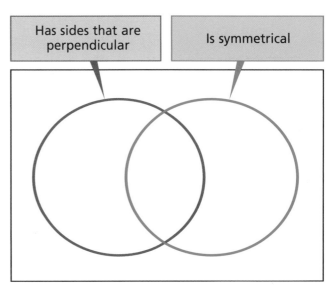

| Has sides that are perpendicular | Is symmetrical |

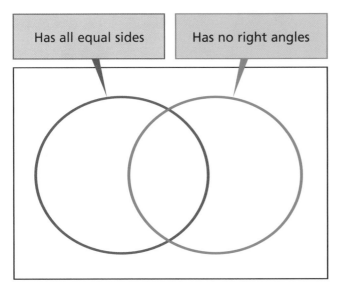

| Has all equal sides | Has no right angles |

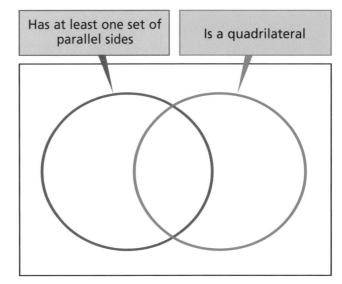

| Has at least one set of parallel sides | Is a quadrilateral |

Explore

Draw a shape to match each description.

1. A quadrilateral with one right angle
2. A symmetrical pentagon
3. An irregular hexagon
4. A quadrilateral with no lines of reflective symmetry

Plug in

A cylinder holds exactly 1 litre. How many millilitres is it holding when it is:

1 half full?   2 a quarter full?   3 three-quarters full?

4 one-tenth full?   5 one-fifth full?   6 two-fifths full?

7 seven-tenths full?   8 four-fifths full?   9 about a third full?

 Power up

Answer these questions.

1 How many faces does a cylinder have?

2 What shapes are the faces of a tetrahedron?

3 How many flat faces does a cone have?

4 How many rectangular faces does a triangular prism have?

5 What shapes are the faces of a cuboid?

6 How many curved edges does a cylinder have?

7 How many edges does a square-based pyramid have?

8 How many vertices does a cuboid have?

9 Which 3-D shape has 6 square faces?

10 True or false? A regular tetrahedron has 6 edges all of equal length.

11 True or false? A hemisphere has one curved face and one circular flat face.

12 How many faces does a hexagonal prism have?

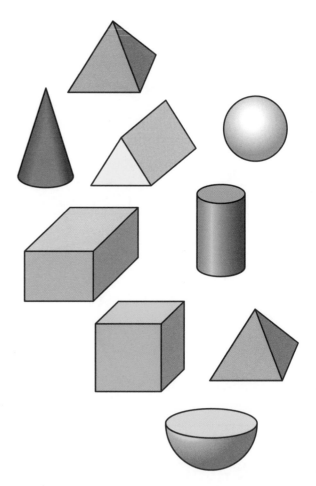

 Chat room

Talk to a partner about the information in the box.

> Euler was a mathematician who discovered that for any 3-D shape that has straight edges and flat faces, if you count up the number of faces, vertices and edges this is always true:
>
> **Number of faces + Number of vertices – Number of edges = 2**

Choose some shapes to check this.

Game play
2 players

You will need: a set of 3-D shapes and two dice.

- Take turns to pick a shape. Place it on the table below.
- Each player rolls a dice to select 'faces', 'vertices' or 'edges'. Each player counts how many of these the shape has.
- The player with the higher number of faces, edges or vertices scores a point. If you both have the same number, both roll the dice again for the same shape.
- The winner is the first player to score 8 points.

Faces   **Edges**   **Vertices**

Explore

Use straws, rods or a construction set to make these 3-D shapes. Name them and describe their properties to a friend.

- Make a shape that has 6 edges of equal length.
- Make a shape that has 2 triangular faces and 3 rectangular faces.
- Make a shape that has 12 edges of equal length.

Recognising properties and sorting shapes

Plug in

1   A regular 2-D shape has equal sides of 6 cm. Work out the perimeter of the shape if it is a:
    a pentagon   b square   c hexagon   d triangle   e octagon   f decagon.

2   Work out the length of each side of:
    a   a regular hexagon with a perimeter of 60 cm.
    b   a square with a perimeter of 16 cm.
    c   an equilateral triangle with a perimeter of 15 cm.
    d   a regular pentagon with a perimeter of 35 cm.

Chat room

Use this diagram to help you explain the words **parallel** and **perpendicular**.

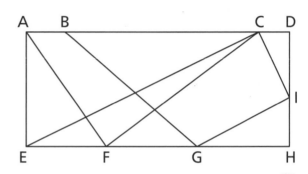

Game play

You will need: cards from PCM 11.
Your teacher will explain the game to you.

How many sides?

Any parallel sides?

Any perpendicular sides?

How many sides?	Any parallel sides?	Any perpendicular sides?	Points
1	yes	yes	50 points
		no	50 points
	no	yes	10 points
		no	1 point
2	yes	yes	5 points
		no	20 points
	no	yes	5 points
		no	10 points
3	yes	yes	1 point
		no	2 points
	no	yes	10 points
		no	12 points

Power up

The vertices of this cuboid are labelled. An edge is described by the letters at each end, e.g. the red line is EH.

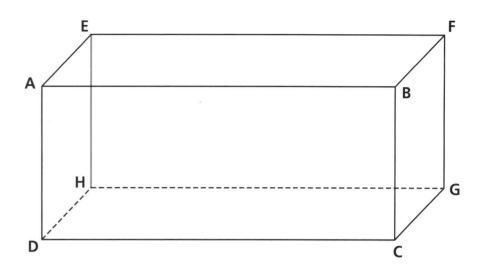

Write whether each of these statements is **true** or **false**.

1 AE is perpendicular to EH.

2 EF is parallel to CG.

3 HD is perpendicular to HG.

4 AB is parallel to HG.

5 AD is perpendicular to EF.

6 EH is parallel to BC.

7 AD is perpendicular to FB.

8 AD is parallel to BC.

9 HD is perpendicular to FG.

10 HD is parallel to FB.

 Explore

Joe is talking about the game opposite.

He says: **It is impossible to score 50 points in one go.**

Do you think he is correct? Explain your answer to a friend.

Drawing 2-D shapes

1 Answer these questions.

a $360° \div 4$ b $90° \times 2$ c $360° - 120°$ d $360° \div 2$

e $90° \times 3$ f $360° - 270°$ g $90° - 45°$ h $360° - 180°$

i $90° + 45°$ j $45° \times 4$ k $90° - 30°$ l $30° \times 4$

2 Are these angles acute, right or obtuse?

a 90°   b 45°   c 30°   d 120°   e 150°   f 10°   g 100°

 Power up

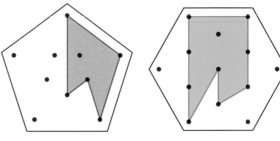

Use the dotted patterns on PCM 12.

You will need: a ruler, a set square and a sharp pencil.

Work with a partner and compare your shapes.

1 On each pentagon pattern draw:

a a hexagon with no parallel sides

b a trapezium

c an isosceles triangle with 3 acute angles

d an isosceles triangle with an obtuse angle

e an irregular pentagon

f a kite

g a scalene triangle

h a decagon.

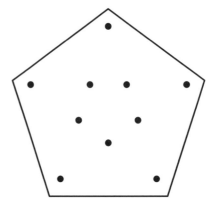

2 On each hexagon pattern draw:

a an equilateral triangle

b a right-angled scalene triangle

c an isosceles triangle with 3 acute angles

d an isosceles triangle with an obtuse angle

e a rectangle

f a trapezium with two right angles

g a pentagon with two right angles

h a quadrilateral whose diagonals are at right angles to each other.

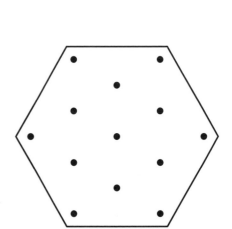

Chat room

Talk to a partner about these instructions. Can you follow them?
To draw an angle of 63°:

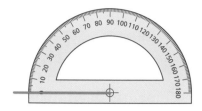

1   Draw a straight line (like the one shown in red).

2   Place your protractor so that
   ● the central cross is at one end of the line
   ● the zero line lies on top of your line.

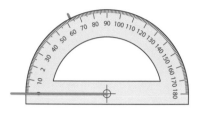

3   Count around from 0° and make a mark at 63°.

4   Remove your protractor and draw a line from your mark
      to the end of your original line.

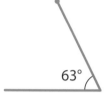

63°

Game play
2 players

● Take turns to pick an instruction from the grid below.
● Both players draw what is written in the instructions and then compare drawings.
● If you have done it correctly, score a point. If not, have another go.
● The winner is the first to score 3 points.

Draw an angle of 156°. Make one of the lines exactly 8 cm long.	Draw an angle of 2°. Make one of the lines exactly 6 cm long.	Draw an angle of 93°. Make one of the lines exactly 7 cm long.
Draw an angle of 163°. Make one of the lines exactly 7 cm long.	Draw an angle of 151°. Make one of the lines exactly 8 cm long.	Draw an angle of 48°. Make one of the lines exactly 10 cm long.
Draw an angle of 37°. Make one of the lines exactly 5 cm long.	Draw an angle of 68°. Make one of the lines exactly 9 cm long.	Draw an angle of 143°. Make one of the lines exactly 4 cm long.
Draw an angle of 148°. Make one of the lines exactly 8 cm long.	Draw an angle of 155°. Make one of the lines exactly 4 cm long.	Draw an angle of 134°. Make one of the lines exactly 5 cm long.

Explore

On dotted paper, draw a shape made from a square and two triangles, but do not
show the joins. Swap with a friend. Can your friend split the shape up again?

Plug in

Chloe has been rolling two dice, finding the product and writing it in a grid.

Write the results marked by letters in the yellow boxes.

×	•	:	∴	::	⁙	⁚⁚
•	1	2		4		
:		4	6			a
∴			b			
::		8			c	
⁙	5		d			e
⁚⁚			f	g		h

 Chat room   Talk to a partner about which of these nets you think would fold to make a cube and which will not.

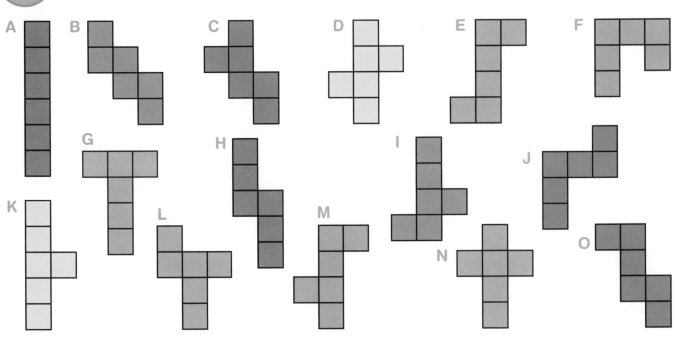

 Power up

What 3-D shape will be made by each of these nets?

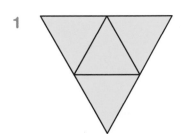

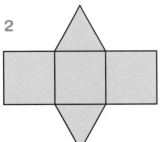

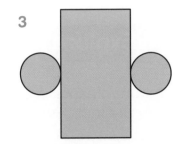

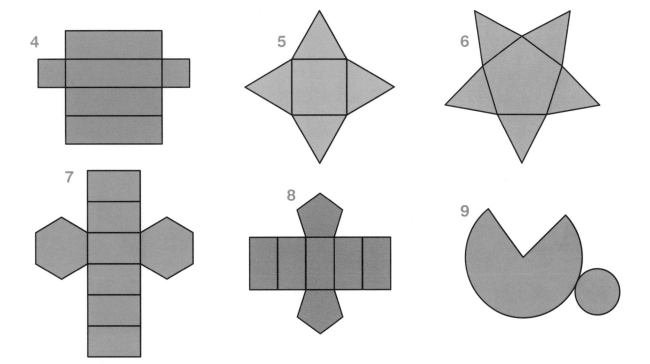

4   5   6   7   8   9

Game play

2 players

You will need: 8 interconnecting equilateral triangles each.

- Take turns to try to make a net of a regular octahedron with your 8 triangles, like this.

- If the shape folds to make an octahedron, score a point.

- The winner is the first player to score 4 points.

(There are more than 10 different possible nets.)

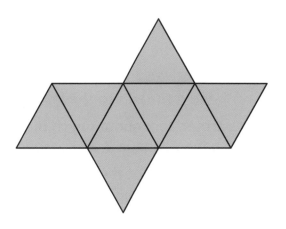

 Explore

Can you draw a net of a dodecahedron?

Draw round a plastic regular pentagon and see if the shape you make will fold to make one dodecahedron.

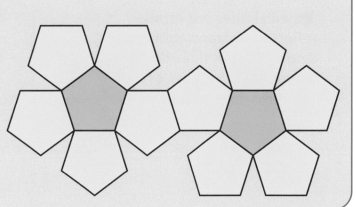

Transforming shapes

 Plug in

Which shape is next in each rotating sequence? Choose from the box and write the letter each time.

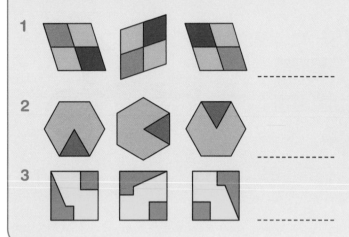

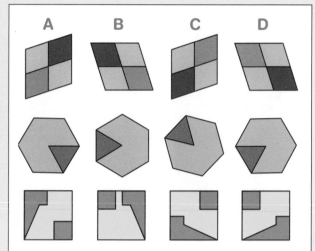

 Chat room

A red shape is changed in three ways, to make the blue shapes. The red shape is:

1   reflected in the dotted line to make shape **A**
2   rotated clockwise through 90° about one of its vertices (corners) to make shape **B**
3   translated 4 squares to the left and 1 square up to make shape **C**.

With a partner, talk about which blue shape is shape **A**, shape **B** and shape **C**.

Look at the lengths of the sides of the shapes and the angles. Do you agree with this statement?

> When shapes are rotated, reflected or translated, the lengths of the sides do not change and the sizes of the angles do not change.

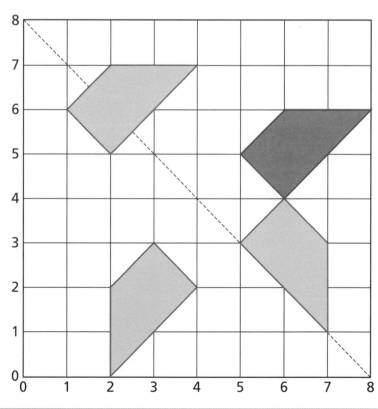

Power up

1   On squared paper, draw a coordinate grid from 0 to 12.
    Plot these points and join them to make a triangle: (2, 2)   (4, 2)   (2, 5)

    Colour the shape red.

2   **a**   Rotate the red triangle from question 1 anticlockwise through 90° about the point (2, 5).
    b   Translate the red triangle 6 squares to the right and 4 squares up.
    c   Reflect the red triangle in the vertical line x = 5.
    d   Reflect the red triangle in the horizontal line y = 7.

3   Reflect the red triangle in the diagonal line x = y.
    (Your teacher will help you with questions 2d and 3).

 Game play
2 players

You will need: squared paper.

● Both players pick two of these coordinate pairs. (2, 4) (0, 2) (5, 5) (6, 6) (4, 5) (2, 7) (1, 1)
● Work together to solve these puzzles. Will your coordinates be the answer?

One vertex of a triangle is at the point (3, 4). The triangle is reflected in the vertical line x = 5. What are the coordinates of the reflected vertex?	One vertex of a square is at the point (2, 2). The square is rotated through 180° about the point (4, 4). What are the coordinates of the rotated vertex?
A hexagon with a vertex at (1, 1) is translated 3 squares to the right and 4 squares up. What are the coordinates of the translated vertex?	One vertex of a pentagon is at the point (4, 2). The pentagon is reflected in the diagonal line x = y. What are the coordinates of the reflected vertex?
An octagon with a vertex at (0, 8) is translated 5 squares to the right and 4 squares down. What are the coordinates of the translated vertex?	One vertex of a triangle is at the point (1, 3). The shape is rotated clockwise through 90° about the point (2, 2). What are the coordinates of the rotated vertex?

 Explore

Jo wants to make a pattern with identical tiles.
She does not want to have any gaps. Which of these tiles could she use?

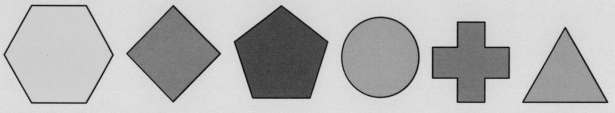

Explain your reasoning to a partner.